The Wonky Donkey

For my mum,
and all the people who have helped me
over the years: family, friends and mentors.
Thank you.
– Craig Smith

To my precious Mum, Dad and aunt Wren ...
your love, support and inspiration fuels my creative journey
and makes all of me smile and sing. With big-fat gratitude
for keeping me tuned to the magic and humour of life.
– Katz Cowley

This edition published in the UK in 2018 by Scholastic Children's Books
Euston House, 24 Eversholt Street, London NW1 1DB
A division of Scholastic Ltd
www.scholastic.co.uk
London – New York – Toronto – Sydney – Auckland – Mexico City – New Delhi – Hong Kong

First published in 2009 by Scholastic New Zealand Limited
Text copyright © Craig Smith, 2007
Illustrations copyright © Katz Cowley, 2009
The moral rights of Craig Smith and Katz Cowley have been asserted.

ISBN 978 1407 19557 5

5 7 9 10 8 6
Papers used by Scholastic Children's Books are made
from wood grown in sustainable forests.

The Wonky Donkey

By Craig Smith

Illustrations by Katz Cowley

SCHOLASTIC

I was walking down the road
and I saw ...

a donkey,

Hee Haw!

And he only had three legs!

He was a
wonky donkey.

I was walking down the road
and I saw a donkey,

Hee Haw!

He only had three legs ...

and one eye!

He was a **winky** wonky donkey.

I was walking down the road
and I saw a donkey,

Hee Haw!

He only had three legs,
one eye ...

and he liked to listen to country music.

Yee Haa!

He was a honky-tonky
winky wonky donkey.

I was walking down the road
and I saw a donkey,

Hee Haw!

He only had three legs,
one eye,
he liked to listen to country music ...

and he was quite tall and slim.

He was
a **lanky**
honky-
tonky
winky
wonky
donkey.

I was walking down the road
and I saw a donkey,

He only had three legs,
one eye,
he liked to listen to country music,
he was quite tall and slim ...

and he smelt really, really bad.

He was a **stinky-dinky** lanky honky-tonky winky wonky donkey.

I was walking down the road
and I saw a donkey,

Hee Haw!

He only had three legs,
one eye,
he liked to listen to country music,
he was quite tall and slim,
he smelt really, really bad ...

and that morning he'd got up early
and hadn't had any coffee.

He was a **cranky**
stinky-dinky lanky
honky-tonky
winky wonky donkey.

I was walking down the road
and I saw a donkey,

Hee Haw!

He only had three legs,
one eye,
he liked to listen to country music,
he was quite tall and slim,
he smelt really, really bad,
that morning he'd got up early
and hadn't had any coffee …

and he was always getting up to mischief.

He was a **hanky-panky** cranky stinky-dinky lanky honky-tonky winky wonky donkey.

I was walking down the road
and I saw a donkey,

Hee Haw!

He only had three legs,
one eye,
he liked to listen to country music,
he was quite tall and slim,
he smelt really, really bad,
that morning he'd got up early
and hadn't had any coffee,
he was always getting up to mischief ...

but he was quite good looking!

He was a **spunky** hanky-panky cranky
stinky-dinky lanky honky-tonky winky wonky donkey!

I was walking down the road
and I saw a donkey ...

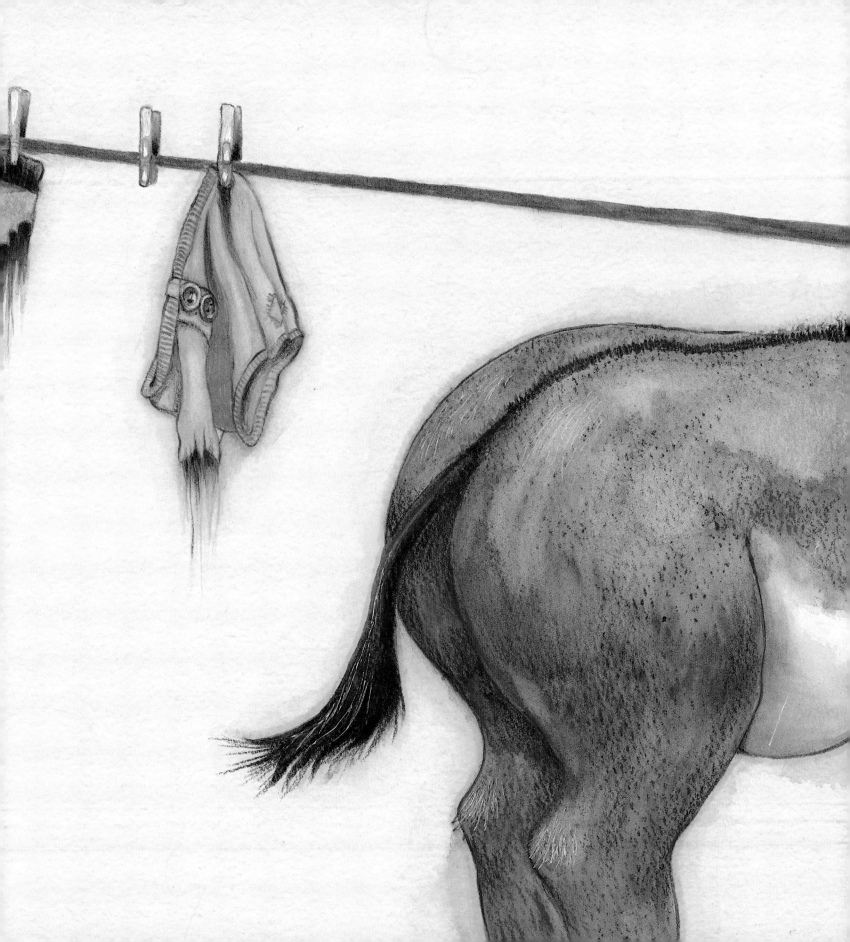